Introduction

Not fully edited.

MY NAME IS PERFECTION. GUN SHOTS BIRTH ME, AND POVERTY RAISED ME. UNEDUCATED PEOPLE ARE ALL I KNOW. PAIN AND SORROW IS ALL I SEEK DAILY. A YOUNG WOMAN WITH ENOURMOUS SHOES TO FILL. IN TOO DEEP AND SCARED THAT I MAY NEVER DIG ME OUT. A POET STUCK IN HELL AND I HOPE I CAN GO TO HEAVEN IN THE NEXT LIFE. THE GUYS FUCK ME AND THROW ME AWAY BUT GOD PICKS ME UP AND MOTIVATES ME TO ACCOMPLISH ALL MY GOALS. AS THE BLOOD DRIPS FROM MY MOUTH, I DRINK A SIP OF WATER AND GET BACK TO WORK. TIME WAITS FOR NO ONE.

Remorseful

Dear GOD, my name is remorse.

I am remorseful through the eyes of me but who I am when I hesitate to pick up your book and read the word.

The word that can heal my mind, my pain, and strengthen my will to forgive the lady who you blessed me inside her.

I'm constantly blaming my mother and my peers who have done me wrong but instead I need to put on my big boy pants and grow up.

But God my biggest problem is to stop believing that the world is against me

The almighty remorse has held in so much blood. Not the blood that runs through my entire body, but the blood that needed to exist. It represents my past that holds me at night and tucks me in, but always stays out of sight.

Dear GOD if I had one wish I would ask if I could love who remorse is.

Instead of waiting for men to love my smile, my poetry, my determination, my skin color, my voice, and my body weight...

Remorse needs to focus on who she is because her name should be Darika not remorse.

"Dirty Laundry"

Ripped clothes: thrown to the front seat as I watched my life flash through my eyes. Kisses all over my back. His hands massaged my breast like he was a caged animal who had just been released. My ribs in knots.

"The Beginning"

It all started when he asked if I wanted a massage. I was young and naïve, and I wanted just to feel the emotion of love; I answered yes with little caution in my voice. We drove to the nearest park where I lived as a little girl. I began to think of Ky, the boy I desperately wanted to be with. The horny ass man leaned over and tried to kiss me; his breath had an odor that turned my tummy green. I refused his kiss, and the rage began. He pinned me down in the back seat of his car and he began to choke me. He said that if I kissed him, he would stop. I still refused, being the little radical, I thought I was. I continued to grab my dirty laundry until he gave in and let me go. Terrified and angry I told him to drop me off at a friend's house. He was pissed, like the devil was trapped in his soul. He asked me why I didn't let him have sex and I responded that I was only expecting a massage.

"Dirty Laundry"

I just regret ever being in love with Ky. Missing him, and craving his love and affection was haunting me. I acted out and searched for others to give me the love I wanted from him. He would tell me he loves me but then he said he had a girlfriend. The whole time he was telling me he didn't want a relationship, only relations. Now I'm still, feeling like this whole relationship is dirty, and I need to do laundry. I feel like dirty underwear; worn so many times but washed only temporarily. Dirty laundry all over my body because I didn't have time to wash the lies and pain out of my clothes.

Rough

Skin tough not smooth but rough

Tears holding back because I'm grown and that isn't allowed

A person can't cry isn't that rough

Abandon by my own mother

Sex, money, weed, and drugs is the only thing that loves her;

rough

Having sex thinking one day just one day he'll wake up and

be mines

Well guess what I woke up with the condom inside me

I guess I was the only one who woke up

Isn't it rough?

To sleep but be wide awake at the same time

It's rough when the pursuit of happiness doesn't exist

anymore

Having feelings for a coworker I just want to be his old lady

but he's older and he wants to be somewhere else

Now isn't that rough?

It's tough when the siblings you once knew doesn't know

you anymore

It's tough and rough when blood drips from your ass and

you don't have money to see a doctor

Life is rough

To sit and wish for something that may never come true

because you're too stuck on guys.

Looking for emotional intelligence and the will to be alone

I sit and wonder what my life would be like if I could focus

on helping myself and not helping the world!

Trying to figure out what's my purpose in this rough place I was born in called life?

To feed off negative energy but to push and seek positive energy doesn't match

I just want to feel loved

I wonder if I can continue living if I never ever receive real and affectionate love.........

"DREAMS ARE FOR SUCKAS"

TO SLEEPWALK, CONTINUOUSLY THINKING ABOUT THE AMERICAN DREAM

WHAT IS THE AMERICAN DREAM?

WHEN YOU DON'T FEEL AMERICAN IN REALITY

THE COLOR PURPLE STANDS OUT LIKE A DETAILED

ARTIFACT OF HARRIET TUBMAN

"THE WOMAN WHOM PEOPLE ARE DISGRACED FOR

HER TO BE ON OUR CURRENCY"

THE SLANG GUNNED DOWN LIKE A MEANINGLESS

LIFE ALL BECAUSE OF DIS=CRIMINATION

IMMIGRANTS FEEL RIGHT AT HOME WHILE I FEEL

LEFT ALONE!

"DREAMS ARE FOR SUCKAS"

WHEN YOUR BLACK PEN IS YOUR SUPPORT

SYSTEM BECAUSE THE GOV= FEELS LIKE THEY

SUPPORTED ENOUGH OF BLACK POOR NIGGAS

DID I ASK TO DREAM?

ANSWER IS NO!

JUST LIKE I DIDN'T ASK TO LIVE IN A HOODLUM

SOCIETY WITH AN INFECTED ENVIRONMENT

MAKING GAMES TO KILL INNOCENT BLACK

PEOPLE WHEN THERE IS BARELY ANY "BLACKS"

LEFT

TO PERSUADE THE POOR THEY'RE NOT WORTH

"TOP NOTCH" EDUCATION STATUS, TO SIT IN A

CLASSROOM WITH EDUCATORS WHO WEREN'T

TRAINED NOR INTERESTED IN SAVING THE GROUP

BLACK LIVES

DRAINED BY LIFE'S POINT OF VIEW I NEED A

PERMENANT SPOT ON THE VIEW

THE DISCUSSIONS WOULD BE WHY BLACK LIVES

MATTERS WHEN AN AK47 BLOWS THE SLIGHT

KNOWLEDGE WE HAVE LEFT.

"WORK HARD PLAY HARD"

UNTIL DEATH APPEARS ON YOUR BED SIDE

DREAMS ARE FOR SUCKAS (WHEN YOUR GREATNESS IS YOUR ENEMY AND LEADS YOU TO YOUR GRAVE SITE)

THUG PARADISE: TUPAC WAS KILLED BECAUSE HE DREAMED AND CONQUERED BUT POWER LED HIM TO REST

NOTICE EACH BLACK PERSON WHO STOOD FOR MORE THAN VIOLENCE LIKE "CHANGE" DIED AND SOCIAL MEDIA RULED IT A SUICIDE INSTEAD OF A HOMICIDE.

EQUALITY ONLY STANDS FOR IMPORTANCE WHEN DEBATING ABOUT MATHEMATICS AND WHITE PROBLEMS

DREAMS ARE FOR SUCKAS WHEN YOU DREAM YOUR SKIN WAS ANOTHER COLOR JUST SO YOU CAN LIVE OUT YOUR FULL POTENTIAL.

DRUG

DRUG CAN BE THE LIQUOR YOU DRINK TO BE CONSIDERED CHILL BECAUSE ON AN EVERYDAY BASIS YOU'RE SYMBOLIZED AS THE BAG LADY.

DRUG CAN BE THE TYPE OF GUYS YOU INVOLVE YOURSELF AROUND.

"THE SMOOTH FULL OF SHIT GAME THEY SPIT".

THE SEXUAL FEELING/SENSATION THEY LEAVE YOU WITH AND!!! THE ATTENTION THEY PRESENT IS LIKE A CHAIN OF COMMAND!

DRUG CAN BE THE CIGARETTES YOU SMOKE TO FILL YOU UP WITH THE NUTRITION YOU NEED TO SURVIVE.

THE HUNGER OF THE FITNESS!

THE HURT AND PAIN YOUR MOUTH ENDURES BECAUSE THE DENTIST IS COSTLY.

THE THOUGHT OF MONEY BEING LOST AND NEVER FOUND.

THE FEELING OF DYING WITHOUT HAVING THE CHANCE TO SAVE HUMANITY.

DRUG CAN BE THE LIFESTYLE!

THE WEED SMOKER WHO WOULD SMOKE SO HEAVENLY YOU WOULD THINK SHE WAS A HIPPIE FROM 1971.

THE DRUG THAT SHE TELLS HERSELF IS BALANCING HER LIFE BUT ACTUALLY ESTABLISHED A CHEMICAL UNBALANCE IN HER BRAIN.

DRUG CAN BE THE BURDEN OF A PAST THAT WASN'T SO BAD BUT STILL EATS HER UP LIKE A TIGER HUNTING FOR FOOD.

THE DANGEROUS LIFESTYLE IS DETERMINED TO BE SHAMEFUL WHEN YOU WOKE UP AND DON'T KNOW THE PURPOSE.

LIFESTYLE CAN BE THOSE WHO SERVE AND PROTECT BUT WOULD BETRAY YOU.

LIKE THE COMPANY DORITOS PERSUADES

IT'S CUSTOMERS THEY BOUGHT A FULL BAG OF CHIPS WHEN THE BAG IS HALFWAY EMPTY.

THE MIND SET COULD BE A DRUG TOO WHEN ALL YOU KNOW IS "HUSTLE AND FLOW".

DRUG CAN BE CONSIDERED BROOKLYN EVEN WHEN MY NAME IS A DRUG BECAUSE I'M ADDICTED TO FALSE IDENTIFICATION.

DRUG CAN EVEN BE YOURSELF WHEN YOU'RE AFRAID OF WHOM YOU ARE BECAUSE "SOCIETY IS AFRAID OF YOU".

Fifty Shades of Black

The scenery doesn't always have a courageous ending.

The scars on the face of "me"—which I'm not sure that I am—are the same scars on my entire body.

Can you imagine being beaten by the rain and society's view of dark-skinned women?

There is the bold symbolism to treasure the women who are slightly fifty shades lighter than I.

But then again, I still haven't figured out who I am.

Today is Thursday May 14, 2015, and the skies are gray, gloomy, and in a religious aspect I believe GOD is crying on me.

Even though the sky is gray in everyone's eyes I believe the sky is fifty shades of black.

People say black lives matter. I say that dark women are tremendous, and shade shouldn't matter, but then again how can you listen to me when I still don't know who I am?

Even though the lead of my pencil is gray, my perspective is fifty shades of black.

On May 24, 2015, as I helped patrol the event, I felt like I was stationed in the era of the Harlem Renaissance. The expressions were speaking like they had seen a strange wild animal.

I felt ugly all over again; why does society dislike me?

But then again, I don't even know who I am.

The laughs from the whites reminded me of the same grins they gave dancers like Josephine Baker during the Harlem Renaissance.

How can I love my skin when society has called me black like the ink from my pen?

How can you love the skin GOD gave you if society makes you feel like your skin was a curse instead of a precious gift?

The skin heals once the skin has the power not to listen to society anymore.

But what happens when fifty shades of your skin—

But then again, the young woman who's writing this poem doesn't even know who she is.

Each time I settle for love and affection through sex my vagina loses a shade, but my skin remains fifty shades of black.

Simple things

Naughty by nature only noticed when she is clothed less

Perfection of the simple things in life but settles for less than what she deserves

Pushed against the wall, hair pulling, and rough sex is all she receives

She wants to be loved, someone to love her inner beauty

Tears on her pillows, detached sins all over her dark body;

she washed her skin over and over but she's still dirty

Clothes, ripped off her body; she remembers being raped

because she cried to her friend about the SIMPLE THINGS

He dosed her with signs of care, but it was false

He knew what he wanted, and she was blind to the reality,

and the events that occurred previously because she wanted

the simple things in life

To lay on the beach with a gentleman was false

For someone to see me beyond the bed sheets

Don't caress my body caress my mind

I needed time to disrupt myself but instead I was caught up

trying to have the SIMPLE THINGS in life

To exist in a world that belittles women, a generation who

cares more about sex than education

My mind has been raped over and over I can barely think clearly

I wake, eat, and sleep THE SIMPLE THINGS; but what happens when the SIMPLE THINGS don't sleep, eat, and wake me?

Do simple things really exist or is it just a fable?

Could I learn how to love myself like a motherless child who grew out of her insecurities?

Or will I stay the same and continue to search for the SIMPLE THINGS even though I haven't completed the search for finding myself?

Isolation will be the only way to find myself, and the simple things are my desire, and the will to keep living this completed life!

Free write

TEARS AREN'T REALLY TEARS THEIR RAINDROPS

CRIES AREN'T REALLY CRIES THEIR EMOTIONS

SCREAMS ARE NOT REALLY SCREAMS THEIR
ATTENTION-SEEKERS

BEING TWENTY YEARS OF AGE, I'M NOW TRYING
TO FIND A WAY OUT OF HELL

ADOLESCENCE YEARS "SAD"

TEENAGE YEARS "SAD"

TWENTIES ARE GOING TO BE FULL OF JOYMENT

THE POET WHO BROKE OUT OF HER SAD SHELL

SHE'S MOTIVATED TO KILL ALL THE VOICES IN
HER HEAD

THE POET WHO WILL GRADUATE FROM COLLEGE;

AND ADOPTED BEAUTIFUL CHILDREN

THE POET WHO STOPPED LAYING IN SORROW AND

IS NOW LAYING IN GRINDS AND HOPE

THE POET WHO STOPPED CRYING BECAUSE TEARS

ARE NOT REALLY TEARS THEIR RAINDROPS

CRIES ARE NOT REALLY CRIES THEY'RE EMOTIONS

SCREAMS ARE NOT REALLY SCREAMS THEY'RE

ATTENTION SEEKERS

Independence; Ride to Paris

Sovereignty, self-government, self-rule, and freedom "the
poor little black girl with nappy hair," run down, one pair of
jeans, and sorrow taboo mark symbol on her back

Raised by a hero who was a single father who emboldened independence inside of Brooklyn

Poverty caused an extreme amount of devotion and cries for the "new generation" a wise man named 2pac said "I am society's child". "This is how they made me and now I am saying what's on my mind and they don't want that". "This is what you made America".

These influential words reminded me of my current situation; begins with a black queen and her lost spirit weakened by loss of hope caused by a dead-beat mother; selfish, wicked, and evil

If she had the chance, she probably would have aborted me

As I'm riding to Paris a young man sits beside me, the invisible queen and tells his surviving story

The story shocks me, kept me up that night and taught me there are more incredible people out there with my current situation

The heart murmur I previously had re-entered my body as he described the painful heart surgery

The young man taught me to not let broken bones, painful scars, sleepless nights, the ability to lose the definition of trust; people have continuously left behind an unbearable past and God helps those who fight through the war to be helped at the end

The term eye for an eye reminds me of the brain washed society we live in

You're more than an eye for an eye because I can sense the lion who wants to help his baby lion

I'm referring to the world

Independence I learned to turn to poetry because this method

is the only thing I'll always have

My current situation includes temporary relationships,

family members, friendships, and temporary love I receive

This ride to Paris let me clear my head from depression,

loneness, presidential problems, crying babies, abandoned

children, disabled people, and the list is continuous

I speak to the empty room that supposed to hold a hundred

people, but I block them out because I fear "they won't

believe I am a poet"

Insecurities killed the cat and Brooklyn continues her ride to

Paris as the young guy tells her another surviving story

I am the motherless young woman with an empty heart

I am a young black woman who has nightmares of her

cousin forcing sex on her

The woman who pushes herself everyday as she opens her eyes like a woman pushing heroin in her arms with an infected needle. I am trapped in a square box living in darkness

The term darkness is what encouraged my independence because I was fighting to love myself and love the woman who births me

The ride to Paris describes my future growth from a nappy black girl to an outstanding young black woman

INDIA: THE GOLDEN FLOWER

VERY RARE FOR BROOKLYN TO BECOME ATTACHED TO ANYONE

THIS PURE SOUL REMINDS ME OF A MOTHER

BROOKLYN NEVER HAD

THE INSPIRATION SHE GIVES TO HER WOULD BE

WORTH A HUNDRED CANCER PATIENTS BEATING

CANCER

A RELATIONSHIP STRONGER THAN HURRICANE

KATRINA AND COULD NEVER BE BROKEN

MRS. GREENE AND INDIA BROKE THE SILENT CRY

INSIDE OF BROOKLYN

SHE OPERATED ON THE BODY OF A LOST

TEENAGER AND GRANTED MY LOVE AND FAITH IN

POETRY

SHE BELIEVED IN BROOKLYN WHEN BROOKLYN

DIDN'T EVEN KNOW WHO SHE WAS

EXCEPT SHE KNEW SHE WAS DIFFERENT AND

HATED ON THE SAME TIMELINE

EVEN KNOW WE HAVE DIFFERENT BLOOD

RUNNING THROUGH OUR VEINS

DIFFERENT SKIN COLOR

GREW UP IN DIFFERENT NEIGHBORHOODS

AND DIFFERENT CHARACTERISTICS YOU'RE STILL

BROOKLYN'S POETRY MOTHER

A HERO WITHIN A MOTHER

CRAYOLAS ARE USEFUL WHEN DESCRIBING

BEAUTIFUL PROTRAITS NOT HUMAN BEINGS

THE LOVE BROOKLYN HAS FOR HER DOESN'T LIE

ON A NUMBER LINE NOR IN A PRESENT CATEGORY

BECAUSE IT RARE

LIKE A RARE/CANCEROUS INFECTION/TUMOR

INDIA THE HEROIC MOTHER LIES IN THE HEART OF

A WONDEROUS YOUNG BLACK WOMAN'

WHO'S SEARCHING FOR A KEY TO HER MOTHER'S

LOVE…...?

INNOCENT

VIDEO GAMES OH HOW I LOVED VIDEO GAMES

THINKING HOW PEOPLE NEVER KNOW THE

SMALLEST THINGS COULD HAVE THE BIGGEST

IMPACT ON YOUR GROWTH IN LIFE

BEING YOUNG DOESN'T CHANGE THE SHIT YOU

DO; THE CRUEL SHIT YOU BRING INTO THE WORLD

AFFECTS HUMANITY

THE FIRST TIME I WAS FORCED TO GIVE ORAL SEX
WAS AT THE AGE OF THREE BY MY OLDER COUSIN

AS HE PLAYED A VIDEO GAME, HE PUT HIS PENIS
IN MY MOUTH AND PROCEEDED TO WIN THE
VICTORY LAP

I DIDN'T COMPREHEND THE MEANING OF ORAL
SEX UNTIL I WAS MUCH OLDER

THE SLAM AND NUT FALLING FROM MY MOUTH
AND THE DISTURBING GAGGING,

HIM FORCING (PUSHING MY HEAD UP AND DOWN)

SO YOUNG AND THROWN TO THE WOLVES. I THINK
MY FAMILY WAS OUT TO GET ME SINCE BIRTH

THIS SAME OLDER COUSIN DOESN'T KNOW HOW
HURTFUL IT IS TO LOOK INTO HIS ROUND EYES

HE WAS A TEEN WHO CONTRIBUTED TO THE RUIN
OF MY LIFE

WHEN A BOY ASKED ME TO PERFORM ORAL SEX
ON HIM, I THINK ABOUT WHAT MY COUSIN DID TO
ME

GOOD GIRLS ARE NO FUN AND BAD GIRLS ARE NO
GOOD (I'M A SYMBOL OF GOOD AND BAD NOW)

THE DEVIL ALL OVER ME AND EVEN HE'S TRYING
TO SLEEP WITH ME

MARCUS

TRUTH IS I ALWAYS FELT LIKE YOU COULD DO
BETTER THAN I

NOT ECONOMICALLY, NOT MENTALLY, BUT
SEXUALLY AND PERFECTIONANTLY

THE FIRST MEETING WITH YOU I KNEW YOUR

ACTION WAS FUCKING AND THE STORY ENDED

TRYING TO GRASP EVERY MOMENT WITH YOU I

END UP FUCKING IT UP

NICK IS RIGHT THE MADNESS IN THE ATMOSPHERE

COMES FROM BROOKLYN WANTING HER KING

IF YOU SIT BACK AND COMPREHEND MY TRUE

FEELINGS FOR YOU

YOU WOULD HAVE FIGURED OUT I WOULD RUN A

THOUSAND MILES TO ASSIST YOUR EVERY NEED

I ALWAYS WANTED TO BE THE ONE WHO MAKES

SURE YOU ACCOMPLISH YOUR GOALS AND LIVE

OUT YOUR DREAMS

BE INTIMATE WITH YOU, SATISFY YOUR HUNGER,

MOTIVATE YOU, BE THE LOVE OF YOUR LIFE, AND

CHERISH YOU

MOST DEFINITELY THANK YOUR BEAUTIFUL

MOTHER FOR BIRTHING YOU

SOMETIMES I LASH OUT AT YOU BECAUSE I 'NEED

YOU'

I KNOW I FUCKED UP BY FUCKING YOU BECAUSE

THAT DIDN'T SHOW THE DOPE POET YOU GOT TO

KNOW NOW

IT SHOWED THE HOPELESS YOUNG GIRL THAT

EVERYONE MAY KNOW

I GUESS THAT IT FELT LIKE A HIT AND RUN

SITUATION

IF I COULD TAKE IT BACK I WOULD, THEN I

WOULDN'T FEEL SO USELESS AND DIRTY

YOU'RE VIBE STRONG LIKE A HOMELESS MAN

THAT SMELLS SOAPLESS

IF I SHOWED YOU NOT ALL HOES ARE FOR SALE,

WOULD YOU FALL HARD ON A HILL TOP OR,

WOULD IT BE THE SAME, I PUT IN ALL THE WORK

AND YOU GAIN

RECENTLY I TOOK THE TIME TO WRITE MY TRUE

FEELINGS INSIDE

ONLY IF YOU WERE THE LINELESS PAPER I'M

WRITING ON

IF SO, I WOULDN'T FEEL SO NERVES INSIDE I'LL

FEEL RIGHT AT HOME

A SMELL THAT OF CONTINUENCE, REGULAR LOVE
NOT TEMPORARY

I BLAME MYSELF FOR GETTING MAD AT YOU LIKE
YOU CAN READ MINDS I GUESS CRIES TURN INTO
ANGER

THE FEELING OF LOSING YOU IS LIKE STRENGTH,
WILLINGNESS WITHOUT FAITH

HOPE I GUESS THIS TERM IS REPHRASED BECAUSE
I KNOW I WANNA BE THE WOMAN WHO BLOWS
YOUR MIND AWAY

I TELL MYSELF MAYBE I SHOULD BURY ALL
FEELINGS FOR YOU AND LET IT SWIM/FLOW IN
THE SEA LIKE THE MOVIE THE NOTEBOOK
HONESTLY TO STOP TALKING TO YOU IS LIKE
LOSING MY HEART AND NEVER RETRIEVING
ANOTHER

YOU'RE ONE OF A KIND LIKE THE GUY WITH A LEAP YEAR BIRTHDAY OR LIKE THE STATUE OF LIBERTY

THE IMPORTANCE SYMBOLIZES THE EARTH SPAN THAT'S HOW MUCH YOU'RE PRESENCE IS NEEDED IN MY LIFE

I WONDER HOW MUCH I'M NEEDED IN YOURS

The hero within the father

A hero is more than a four-letter word that describes a phenomenal person who excelled in the field of saving others

A hero within the father describes my FATHER (A man who raised three beautiful but split personalities on his own)

A hero symbolizes and honors a remarkable man who fought for peace, education, and to love his children.

Peaceful thoughts that run in a head of a heroic black man; but to fight the addiction drunk of sick and wicked negativity/my father fought society's myth that every Black Men is a dead-beat father.

Through my eyes the daughter I learned to see the end of the war before the war actually comes to an end

Because of my hero I learned to seek more of life than colors, friends, violence, sex, babies, and revenge on a simple-minded mother.

The man who taught me to take my first step into this world and to adult hood

The hero who disciplines values was like a commander but loved us like the black panthers loved to fight for change

The hero who told me black is beautiful and to love yourself before you can love anyone

50 SHADES OF BLACK inspired by my heroic father because he told me despite the color of your skin you are a beautiful child inside and out (you know within the body; kinda like the heart that makes you want to be kind to the world that has cruel people)

The hero who doesn't want anything from me but to accomplish all my goals and continue to educate myself; one of his quotes is a wise person would learn something new every day, don't ever stop learning. The reality is my biggest goal is to give my father what he needs because he has given me the precious gift that could never expire which is LOVE

My father is my best friend, provider, father, mother, and the person who is my biggest inspiration.

THE HERO WITHIN THE FATHER

My father is irreplaceable because no one is as strong

minded and strong physically like my father

The temptation to love yourself because your dad loves you

like no other

My father is the true definition of a hero within.

Used trash bag

DISOWNED, THROWN AWAY LIKE BRENDA THREW

AWAY HER BABY. DISOWNED LIKE A RELIGIOUS

FATHER DENOUNCED HIS RELATIONSHIP WITH HIS

DAUGHTER FOR BEING GAY. REJECTED FROM

SOCIETY BECAUSE OF MY UNBLEMISHED DARK

SKIN, PLUMB BIGNESS, MY SERIOUS FACE

EXPRESSION, MY ABSTRACT MIND SET TO CHANGE

SOCIETY'S VIEWS, MY LONELINESS, MY PERSPECTIVE OF MEN, BUT MY FAILURE TO LOVE ME (TO ACCEPT ME, TO BOND WITH ME, AND TREAT ME LIKE A HUMAN, WHICH SOCIETY DOESN'T). A TRASH BAG IS DEFINED AS A PLASTIC BAG PUT INSIDE A BIN TO HOLD THE WASTE AND KEEP THE CONTAINER CLEAN; I FEEL LIKE A USED TRASH BAG, DIRTY INSIDE AND OUT. I LET UNSOPHISTICATED MEN/BOYS TAKE AVANTAGE OF MY TREASURE. I LET THEM TIE MY SOUL INTO A KNOT, RIP MY VAGINAL AREA INTO MANY SORE PARTS, AND DISSARANGE MY KIND HEART INTO A DEVIL'S CRY FOR HELP. THE VOICES OF ALL THE MEN LAUGHING AND SMIRKING AT THE TRASH LADY, I JUST WANT TO CURL UP AND WHEEP. A WET TRASH BAG FULL OF SMELLY FOOD, OLD JUICE AND VEGTABLE BROTH, AND ETC. THE

WOMAN WHO SETTLED FOR GUYS WHO ONLY
WANTED A CERTAIN PART OF THE TRASH BAG
INSIDE OF THE PRIMARY BODY PART, MY MIND. A
CRY FOR HELP. THE TRASH BAG ENDED UP IN A
RIVER FULL OF PETTY SITUATIONS AND WASTE.
FLOODING, TRYING TO SURVIVE THE ENORMOUS
AMOUNT OF WATER, THE TRASH BAG RESTED ON A
ROCK LOCATED IN THE MIDDLE OF THE RIVER,
TRYING TO USE A MODERN COMPASS TO LOCATE
HER NEXT STEP. THE BAG SITS AND STARES AT ALL
THE WASTE

WHO AM I?

WHO AM I? THE WOMAN WHO PREDICTS AND SEES
HER FUTURE BUT CAN'T RETRIEVE HER REALITY.

WHO AM I? THE WOMAN WHO TEARS COME OUT OF HER SKIN HAIRS LIKE THE INTENSE ODOR FROM DRINKING ALCOHOL.

WHO AM I? THE WOMAN WHO IS SCARRED BY HER OWN NIGHTMARES, THE ONE WHO SCARES HERSELF INTO FRIGHTNESS LIKE FREDDY KUGAR. WHO AM I? THE WASHED-UP SISTA WHO IS CLEANSED THE WORLD WITH SOAP, WATER, FAITH, AND FUNDS BUT LEFT WITH SACRIFICES RUNNING DOWN THE DRAIN.

WHO AM I? THE ONE WHO KNIFE CUTS ARE DEEP AND CAN BE COMPARED TO THE THOUGHTS THAT ARE FLOWING THROUGH MY OVERPROTECTIVE BRAIN. CELLS THAT ARE COMPARED TO "WILDLIFE". BLOOD CONTRASTED WITH DEATH "ONCE DEATH APPEARS BLOOD LOSES

EXISTENCE." WHO AM I? THE COURAGEOUS WOMAN WHO ROSE FROM THE CONCRETE? "MAYA ANGELOU"

BUT STILL MISUNDERSTOOD BY THE PHRASE "DECLARATION OF INDEPENDENCE." WHO AM I? THE NICK-NAME LADY-BUG THE WOMAN WHO BIRTH ME WOULD CALL "THE POET" WHEN SHE WAS IN A LAUGHTER MOOD.

IS MY LIFE WORTH LIVING OR IMPORTANT LIKE ECONOMICS? WELL, IF SO "CAN I LIVE" IN JAYZ'S VOICE.

WHO AM I? THE WOMAN WHO FUCKS FOR COMFORT?

SHE WANTS LOVE BUT DUMPED IN THE TRASH LIKE BRENDA'S BABY (TU-PAC'S SONG). WHO AM I?

A SELECTION OF SOCIETY THAT IS SEGREGATED "1950" "WHITE SIDE/BLACK SIDE."

COULD IT BE I WAS BRAINSTORMED AND WRITTEN OUT LIKE AN INFLUENTIAL ESSAY?

WHO AM I? THE WOMAN WHO IS CLOISTERED. STUCK IN 2020 BUT UNABLE TO FUNCTION IN 2015. WHO AM I? THE WOMAN WHO WAS TIED TO THE REAR SIDE OF THE BOAT TITANIC AND DIED INSTANTLY.

WHO AM I? THE MEANINING IS MORE THAN A SHORT QUESTION; THE POET IS SEARCHING FOR AN ANSWER.

WHO AM I IS NOT A RHETORICAL QUESTION?

NOT KNOWING WHO YOU ARE GIVES SOCIETY A SPOT TO KILL YOU IN A HIGH-SPEED CHASE ON THE FREEWAY.

WHO AM I? THE COMEDIAN WHO IS DROWNING IN HER OWN NON-HILARIOUS JOKES. WHO AM I REALLY? I AM POVERTY

MY MASCOT IS HOME OF LACK OF EDUCATION, MALNUTRITION, AND SUBSIDIZED HOUSING.

WHO AM I? HONEY OF THE BEEZ "BITTERSWEET"

Rainbow

Friends call me Darika and some call me Brooklyn, but I refer to myself as Rainbow. I carry my past on my jagged back; stumbling, crawling, falling trying to piece my life together. Lady Rainbow what's wrong? Is it possible to be abused by someone younger than you? I believe anything is possible. At times I would be dreaming of changing the world and next minute I feel unsympathetic, unaccompanied, chills like it were winter; snow for instance becomes my new baby. As I jumped and turned my body with immobility, I noticed my brother in my room, eyes wide like an owl and blood-shot red like he was intoxicated. Lady Rainbow how do you feel about life? I paused then loudly I shouted I hate life. Why does life have to be so firm? I do what I'm supposed to do and still my surroundings include pain and negativity. Thrown at Rainbow like stalwarts and twigs. Be tolerant little one but lady Rainbow just wants someone she can go to when the light to the future is blurry. Being too needy is a criminal act and following in love is as simple as a fairy-tale. Being tied down is a depraved habit, but I continued to act out immoral habits! So, what do Rainbow do now, she's lost, on one-side of her needs to be punished and the other-side is an attention seeker. Is lady Rainbow missing essential appearances or is she meant to be alone?

My Flower

My flower blooms at night when it's time for my head to rest on an indulgent and fluffy pillow. My flower is a man who kisses are as soft as a rose petal. He tells me everything would be okay and to be all I can be even when I disbelieve myself. In the seasons of fall and spring I just want to relinquish. He holds me like a king goes to battle for his queen; like a loyal group becomes legendary like Salt and Pepper. Watching the sunset with my flower is the ideal date. Playing in his hair relaxes my mind from all the things that kills me inside, from the ghosts that haunts me and the friends that betrayed me. What really hurts is the family that is ashamed of me! My flower tells me to do my assigned assignments when I just want to sleep. When I tell my flower I wish I wasn't born and assuring that my mother should have had an abortion. When he hears those words, he instantly looks dead, dried out, like he hasn't had enough water. I try to make him smile even now I'm not happy within. My flower is here for me, so I protect him and water him to show love. (Dedicated to Ky)

I Mean What I Say

When I want something done, I get it finalized. If I tell you I love you I mean what I say! The lips sweet like treats. The kisses on my cheeks from your juicy lips, don't hesitate to kiss me, if I want a kiss, I mean what I say. What's wrong with showing emotions; if I want a hug, I mean what I say. Time waits on no one. So, If I

Want you next to me I mean what I say. If I want to be the odd girl out, then I mean what I say. The polish on my sore and swollen feet symbolizes my love for economics. Don't tell me a lie tells me the truth because I mean what I say. Words are as powerful as actions so do you mean what you say.

Phenomenal Woman (dedicated to Maya Angelou's Poem)

People wonder why I'm quiet during class sessions.

It's because I wasn't made to please everybody.

Stares through the hallway when I pass by.

Long braids swinging from left to right, like time was created from hair. Wanting me to do the erroneous things so they play with my mind. Is this paralleled to spin the bottle? Did the bottle land on dare? Strangers calling me bag lady "yelling out I'm going to hurt my back" (Ms. Badu). But I can handle it because I'm a woman phenomenally. Phenomenal woman that's me. Dazy ducks, white shirt, green sweater, black Nike's. Don't judge a book by its cover! Is it my mean face expressions that run/trembles people? Is it my dark chocolate skin that drives the young men wild but frightens the young girls? The smile I finally showed blew their confidence south. Is it my soft lips that men love to kiss or maybe the fact I have low self-esteem! I have ups and downs; I promise I'll try not to frown. Why, because I'm a woman phenomenally. A phenomenal woman that's me.

"Birthplace"

Separation from the worn I was once connected too. The picture-perfect scenery outsiders believed I lived; like I was raised in a fairytale. Unfortunately, I'm from Los Angeles; home of the unwanted. Black mothers having children at sixteen; and was taught receiving money from the Gov. would help them survive. Black mothers having abortions rapidly because they don't know how to use a condom, or they think they're in

"Love". Black young fathers are thrown in prison because they were trying to chase the American Dream in a negative way. Young men killing each other because of a territory they believe they own, a color they were persuaded to believe is the symbol of who they are and being from a certain territory will keep them alive. The key is to not make the same mistakes our mothers made. I'm from a place where being educated is rare, and unfortunate. Blood trails from our ancestors who tried to fight for our freedom of speech fades loudly but badly into each future generation. Home of the fast money. Disrespecting women, women with no goals or morals. Drugs weakening the minds of my people but they're too blind to notice. Brittle attacks by the ones you love. Secrets lie upon the heart of forgiveness but sides with the darkness to destroy one's peace. I'm from Los Angeles; home of death

"Snakes"

Snakes slithering under the cold waters. Ponds filled with filthy lies that I continuously hear daily. Snakes' kisses are sweet like cotton candy but weak and bitter like old folks. Sex seems to be the only interest; this is my biggest problem. It hurts me in my sleep, it chases me until I can't resist. The snakes I meet always want a taste of my "brown sugar" They plead the fifth and I try to run and hide like hide

and seek. I ask myself why sex wants me so desperately.
Why can't I like a snake without him trying to bite me!
Girls, I use to tell myself I'm not beautiful, I'm fat,
unattractive, so why do these snakes want me? The answer
is the smile I have, the toughness I was taught, the education
I'm willing to learn, and I'm short and thick. The last
characteristic is I have inner beauty. The snakes try to stop
me in my tracks, but I explain to them we come from two
different worlds and where I'm going you may not enjoy. I
have a limit for snakes, becoming another statistic makes me
fear these snakes, so the best thing to do is stay away. My
mind wants to graduate from college and help young teens,
but my heart want love. Trying to juggle the two I panic and
begin to lose control of my next move. One thing I know is I
can't slither with these snakes under cold waters...

Lusting (Dedicated to Ky)

Motionless from the appearance of Ky. Wet dreams, clueless thoughts, shattered words, un-organized vocabulary, and "sloppy seconds". Calling you isn't an option, so my fantasies of Ky is what requires me through the day and night. Legs acting in a pyramid stance and hands massaging the core of you (every inch). Temptation rises high like the sexual thoughts I get when purple haze was the hobby. Lusting for Ky is more than physical activities, an intense and deep conversation with you gives me butterflies and the lust becomes stronger. Ky the questions I always wondered is what describes your soulmate? Weaken by the glare in your eyes and the content from your music I just stare into the stars and vent. The silence in the 4-door car takes place because you make me thought-less. Your cleanliness and odor smells refreshing. If I had one more night to lust about Ky, I would dream of telling you about my true feelings with confidence, not experiencing the feeling of being ashamed. Ashamed of dismissal or mistreatment. I should embrace the thoughts of lusting someone special like you.

My Stuff

I want what belongs to me; I want my stuff back. I was only 14 when I let him hurt my precious stuff. The tenderness, burning, stinging like I was being re-born. Voices in the back of my head saying tell him to stop, I want my stuff back. He was thoughtful to ask if I wanted him to stop; but the bold and tough little girl I was I said no! I want my stuff; I want belongs to me. I want what belongs to me so bad I want the blood to re-enter my body and become clean again. My innocence is gone, and I want it back, it belongs to me. This one girl told me oh you're still a virgin wow I lost mines a long time ago. She made me feel like I was stupid and sick for still having my innocence. As I become full of shame, I really became determined to lose my virginity. I want what belongs to me. The soft and sweet thing it was to be young and innocent. Being so young and smart, always telling myself to keep my legs closed and books open. After he took what was mines, I felt dirty and used. I felt like I did something wrong, and I couldn't change the un-done. As I think about what I did, I beat myself up. I feel like I could have gotten pregnant so why put myself into that! I want what belongs to me! I want that tightness and untouched back. I want my pride back. Once it's gone it's hard to get back. Like someone who lost everything, like someone who screams for forgiveness and peace. My innocence always speaks to me. I want what's mine why is it so hard to find. I just want what I can't have; MY STUFF….

BREAKAGE

FEET SORE FROM WALKING ON EGG SHELLS.

BREAKAGE

HAIR PULLED OUT "NOT FROM HARSH

CHEMICALS" BUT FROM STRESS.

BREAKAGE

ASH TRAYS FILLED WITH A FAMILIAR SMELL FROM

THE NEWPORT CIGARETTE BUTTS.

LUNGS BARELY FUNCTIONING DUE TO THE

AMOUNT OF CIG. I SMOKE AN HOUR.

BREAKAGE

LACK OF SHOESTRINGS TO TIE NOT FROM

ECONOMIC REASONINGS BUT FROM PERSONAL

BELIEFS.

BREAKAGE

DAILY THOUGHTS OF DEATH DUE TO A SLIP AND FALL, BREAKAGE

SOCIETY LEFT ME TO HANG HIGH AND DRY WITH THE REST OF THE SELECTION CALLED "POVERTY" …. BREAKAGE

A FAMILIAR SMELL OF WHAT I CALL HOME IS OLD BLOOD SPOTS, A HOMELESS OLD WOMAN WHO SMELLS DUE TO LACK OF BATHING, AND THE SMELL OF DEAD RATS AND SCREAMS

BREAKAGE

HAIR TIED DUE TO RELAXATION BUT WHO COULD RELAX WHEN THE WORD SYMBOLIZES DARIKA'S IDENTITY.

BREAKAGE

CLOSING STATEMENT: THANK YOU WONDERFUL PEOPLE FOR READING MY STORY. IT TOOK THREE LONG YEARS TO ACTUALLY MEET THE RIGHT PEOPLE TO HELP ME PUBLISH MY BOOK. THESE POEMS EXPRESS THE SITUATIONS AND MISTAKES I TAKE CREDIT THAT I SHOULDN'T HAVE ACTED IN SUCH A MANNER. I'M GROWING EACH DAY TO LOVE MYSELF AFTER BEING CALLED AN UGLY BLACK ASS ANIMAL WHO IS FAT AND UNLOVABLE. GOD HAS LIFTED ME UP AND STANDS WITH ME EACH AND EVERY STEP AND BREATH I TAKE. THE DEVIL WILL NOT BREAK DARIKA BROWN....!

My father is my primary inspiration and my biggest fan:}

Made in the USA
Middletown, DE
05 June 2023

31837172R00036